I0211891

VIA Folios 183

Hunger

Published by Bordighera Press, an imprint of the John D. Calandra Italian American Institute of Queens College, The City University of New York.

25 West 43rd Street, 17ᵗʰ Floor, New York, NY 10036

All rights reserved. Parts of this book may be reprinted only by written permission from the publisher, and may not be reproduced for publication in media of any kind, except in quotations for the purposes of literary reviews.

Library of Congress Control Number: 2025942205

Cover image by Danielle Jones

© 2025, Danielle Jones

VIA Folios 183
ISBN 978-1-59954-238-6

Hunger

Danielle Jones

BORDIGHERA PRESS

Table of Contents

for my mother

I

Variants on a Roman Landscape

Ceprano - 1922

Houses stacked
on hillsides,
shutters drawn
against the sun's first slant.

*

A river rushes over rock—forks into east
and west.

*

Beneath the bluffs, women
wade in the runoff pool,
skirts tied off at the knees.
They wash la biancheria,
smooth the thin cotton
over stones.

*

Olive trees
gnarl the field,
their leaves
offering no shade
from the noon sun.

A boy clambers
over a fence, reaches
the road that runs through town.
He hops
from stone-
to-stone, careful
not to touch
the moss between—
counts *uno, due,*
        uno, due

*

At a street side cafe, a man
with whiskers
shadowing his face
sips his first beer of the evening.
It's too warm. A woman
in a muslin dress
passes, almost smiles.

Dovrebbe essere a casa,
con sua moglie.

Non ho moglie.

*

Streetlamps snap on, shine
on white walls, white
street, a white stone house

a window swung wide:

inside
a pair of night eyes,
watching.

The Spy

Mama never says *watch*
but *if you see*—I take off
my slappy sandals, toes cold
as I sneak up
the marble steps, crouch
on the third-floor landing,
hiding behind a wood panel, peeking
through the carvings, I see

their bodies, pressing together,
his grey wool slacks, her black skirt
rolled so the hem hits
above the knee. The tinny sound
of trumpets whizzing through
the Victrola. When my brother twirls her

I see the black lines of her nylons
running up the center of her
calves. Twisted, they make
her legs seem bowed. The music stops,

leaving only the shuffle
of their soles
against the wood floor. Then
silence. I stare

at her red mouth
until it disappears, obscured
as my brother leans in—

but even then, the afterimage
burns red
and red and red, throbbing
like a heart in my head. I
don't tell. I keep this kiss
for myself.

Sapere Aude

Francesca comes looking for miracles. I come
for the clack/shuffle of his body
limping up the nave. His church shoes shine

under dirt-stiff cuffs, and the wink
of bony ankle between. I scratch
my grin with my best lace gloves, watch

as he crumples his hat in the claw
of his left hand. In his strong right hand,
a pinch of day-old bread. It takes three

hail Marys for him to reach the lamps
the Sisters of the Sacred Heart
just finished filling with olive oil, bits

of rag twisted into wicks. He holds the crust
high above his head, like a host
being transformed into holy sacrament. *Iddio*—

his voice flutters like a pigeon
caught in the cathedral rafters—*posso n'zuppa*
er pane? He bows his head, waits

for an answer. But it's his own voice,
basso profondo, which echoes through
the near empty church in response:

Si, figlio mio, n'zuppa, n'zuppa. He dips his bread
in the warm green oil, leaves
the same way he came in. I feel

full, mirth rising like bubbles
inside me. But then
I look at my sister, her eyes

closed, her body trembling,
lovely as a luna moth, starving
for silk she can't taste.

Pietà

We sit shoulder-to-shoulder, pass
chipped white plates to one another. Papa

pours the last of the wine
and we're all given a thimble full.

We make up stories, raise our voices
to the rafters, try to be louder

than the noon-time news:
strikes, beatings, blacklisted names

crackling through the speakers—
our father's, again, disappearing

in the dust and din. Mama spoons
rust-colored sauce from a dwindling pot,

pushes little bites of the meat she's saved
onto the boys' plates, before they're sent

to lie on their beds, to rest, wait
for better days. Keep them out

of these *cattive strade,* I hear
her say. I see their sock feet

from the hall I'm sent to sweep.
My muscles flex, unflex, flex

again—see the strength
hidden beneath my olive skin.

Abandoned Gardens

Papa wasn't afraid to scavenge. Untangling
weeds, cutting brush, looking for a handful
of prickly greens, wild artichokes, frost-touched
strawberries he'd twist into his monogrammed
handkerchief. Once he found a chicken scratching
the dry dirt of a half-burnt barn. He brought it home
and everybody danced. Even the chicken.

Pietà

Michaelangelo, 1499

Oh, how I wanted her
alabaster skin, her
sculpted breasts, her arms,
strong, folds of robe,
her mountainous curves. Wanted
her knees, parted
and locked, like when
she gave birth, sway back,
sprawled lap, solid
as a tree trunk. Look
at the ruffles
carved in marble,
the ripples, her gathered
gown, flowing
river of stone
cascading down
to her perfect, chisel-
chipped toes. I needed
the cool of her
smooth brow, half-
closed eyes, her *hush, hush*
baby. I did not want
her upturned hand,
empty as why, accepting
empty sky—No. I wanted
the other hand, the one
clinging fiercely,
furiously holding
her dead son.

The First Time I Felt My Body Move

I watched the fishermen
drag the boy up
the muddy bank, his hair
the only thing moving

*

mama made chamomile tea,
while the neighbor
whispered through the steam:
twice the size—
had to slice
the seam of his suit—

I imagined him
split in two,
the fine line
between dressed
and undressed

dropped my cookie
into my cup,
watched it swell

*

the wake, swoon
of flowers, waterfall
of lilies spraying
from his folded
hands, hiding

the thick swallow
of his belly

his blue eyes still
open, dim
as the buttons
on my winter coat

the carpet pooled
around my feet—I ran

*

strum of blood

cobblestone jags
bruising my heels

breath too sharp
to be held,

like smoke—

I ripped
the buttons from my blouse

running
too fast to hear them fall

War Time, and He

names the bunnies after Mussolini's men,
the ones who beat him bloody
when he wouldn't sign their cards. Fingers thick
and itching to break their necks.
He waits. Watches them grow plump.

War Time, and She

cuts slices of potato so thin you can see the sun
of her skin shining through them. One for each
child's tongue, a communion. She says *close
your eyes, pretend it's apple.*

Osvaldo Runs Away to Join the Foreign Legion

He emptied the hope chest
in the night, had the seamstress
cut the cloth into suits, his smile
worth the time it took her
to pick loose the strands
of his sister's tightly stitched
bridal bouquets. Stepping onto

the platform in his crisp, white
three-piece, he was chosen
for the brass band rather
than the front lines. Lucky.

Everybody said so. And on
his right breast pocket,
a delicate something
the seamstress had missed:
bones of a rose, carved
by a restless needle.

February 23, 1944: To Combat the Italian Underground, Hitler Ordered That for Every German Officer Killed Ten Italian Civilian Men Would Be Shot

That morning on the streets
they'd heard the whispers: a German
found—naked—a finger-hole
in his forehead, soft edges, a
trickle of blood. Depressed
skull. Both of his eyes
sunken in cave-mouth
shadows.
No one cared,

but everyone
was scared, scattered
like animals, hoping
they wouldn't be
one of the ones
rounded up
and slaughtered.

When a Potato is More Like a Prayer

He's always home in time
to wring the rabbits' necks
for Sunday supper.

She holds the potato, blunt stone
in her hand. The thick hide
a different kind of animal.

She skins it with short, stiff strokes:
each one a little yelp, but underneath
satisfying white—no blood

soaked papers, no fur, no writhing
guts to untangle. When she finds
a dark one, decay boring holes into flesh,

eyes open and staring, she goes outside
and tosses it back to earth, hoping
for something good to be reborn.

She returns to the kitchen, her one certainty:
whether he returns or not, she'll still have
to put supper on the table.

Timekeeping

1.

Before: waking to his flannel back turning off
his alarm clock, making him warm milk and coffee,
wrapping bread in a flour sack, putting it in his blue
lunch pail. Setting the dinner table when his shoes
stomped the doormat, knowing it was time for bed
when he fell asleep in his chair, radio on, chin on chest,
glasses low on his nose.

2.

By the time she remembered the river, the water
was warm. We carried sloshing buckets to the cellar
to cool. For breakfast, our teeth scraped bread that would
not break. At noon, she hoisted the pot onto the fire, but
when she didn't hear his whistle warbling over cobblestones
she forgot to throw the pasta. Water boiled, raging
then receding, kitchen filling with the ghost of steam.

3.

Hands hide her face. The dress-bowl of her lap sagged
with the weight of my father's alarm clock, smooth steel,
open face set on stout legs, brass arms ambling, slowly
unwinding.

4.

After: the bell that didn't ring, the door that didn't open,
black stretches of night mama knew would end
only when he didn't wake up.

A Year Spent Imagining the Day He Died

Stone wall behind him. An orchard
beyond. He notices an apricot, can tell
the skin is still too thick, its flesh
not yet pushing its boundaries.
He refuses to bend his neck,
to cover his eyes—won't lean
against the wall—but his hands (tied
behind his back) stroke damp peat moss. Soft
as his daughter's hair. *Dolce*
far niente. When it's time,
he hopes a child finds the fruit,
makes the first wish of the season, wishes
for something sweet.

Night Garden

Mama wakes me to help her bury
china, the hydrangeas stippled pink

and blue. We work without words.
Breathe in mulch, wet earth. I see her

shiver through her robe; feel goosebumps
rippling up my arms. If it were morning

we'd lean into the sun. What's left
of the moon winks on the empty face

of plates, gleams like too much milk
in the bowls. She binds each piece

in strips of papa's shirts. I push the bundles
into the ground. My nails fill with dirt, tear,

as I scratch holes for saucers, for the demitasse
cups, delicate as petals pressed inside book pages.

Handfuls of soil whisper over faded cloth. *Our
secret.* I learn to let go, to wait, for the day

we live to harvest bone and all these breakable blooms.

Crypsis

we tried to be transparent/tried not to shine like glass or even salt/
just wanted to take on our surroundings/to let the dirt breathe
through us/to blend in with weeds/ditches/invisibility was a luxury/
unimaginable/unable we tried to be the black in the half-burnt barn/
the black behind our hands our eyelids/to slide down soft as nylons/
not to rip/not to stand out like white/knees/like naked/we wanted
to be the shadow on the midnight shade/to creep home like cats or
to squeeze through pipes/tried to be as closed as our fists/self-con-
tained as barbed wire/ phantom pain/ we were as small as untraceable
as the gods' mistakes/but the more they bombed the more we stood
out/like prayers/no pleading/we were giants scratching the sky of a
razed city/white-ash buildings/cut outs]   sky   [white/ash/every-
where holes/we wanted to be those holes/ instead we filled and filled
until we forgot how to stop filling/how to stop being   [targets]

Storming the Bakery

We learned in history class that bread, or
lack of it, caused the French Revolution,
so no one's surprised when the women,
mama included, storm the bakery
with sticks and stones, kitchen knives,
demand more than their rations. *Everyone
knows the baker makes the Tedeschi
sourdough,* Elsa says. *You see how
his own kids bust the seams of their
winter coats,* another woman hisses—
They shove beignets in their pockets,
fit round loaves in the hollows beneath
their ribs. Maria Grazia pokes a baguette
into the insatiable mouth of her purse. *Polizia!*
the bakers shouts, but no one pays attention.
Giulia's nonna stands by the door, brandishing
her rolling pin. It's almost Christmas
and these women will not be leaving
without the sweet bread that's baking.

Nostra Donna del Cielo

Sirens all night, but in the morning
Mama still made us go to mass.
From down the hill we could see
the spire was gone, smoke
holding its place like phantom pain.

We made our way over rock
crumbled like cookies, over pages
of songbooks, scattered and shredded,
shards of stained-glass crunching
beneath our feet, stabbing our thin soles.
Our church clothes blackened, bodices
pulled over our mouths, noses,
breaths raspy through crisp crepe.

In the apse, still intact but attached
to nothing, the priest stood, lost
in his baggy slacks and sagged neck
t-shirt. He was surrounded by stone
bodies. At his feet, wrapped in black
vestments, Baby Jesus, dimpled legs
and arms captured mid-wriggle.
Joseph, face-down in ashes, hand-
carved marble cracked at the waist.
And there—flat on her back—Mary,

tiny pink toes peeking from the hem
of her gown. She was breathing. I took
off her veil to see the slope of her ribs,
the hollow spot before her abdomen swelled,
flattened, swelled beneath the blue organza.
I could hear my sister crying somewhere

behind me, but I couldn't take my eyes
off her face. Red splotched. Freckled.
Her nose a bit hooked. But her eyes—
I'd never seen her look up. It was like seeing
the inside of a seed, or feeling
that first blush rising.

Mama Said When the War is Over

there will be bread. I pictured the long loaves
we used to tear with our hands, but nothing's
ever that easy. With the Americans come sacks
of flour. She uses only the point of her knife,
but still some spills on the counter. It's smooth
between my fingers, like the talcum powder
nonna hides between stockings and camisoles.
I pinch little mountains in it. When I come home
from school, our big bowl's covered with a tea towel.
I peek beneath, pop a bubble on the doughy surface.
Is it done, Mama? She punches the rubbery moon
right in its middle: everything deflates in the sink hole
her fist leaves. She replaces the checkered towel,
waits for a second rising.

Portrait of a Woman in Kitchen

before morning unties its birds, before heat
pings its way from room to room, her breakfast music
shakes me. half-dreaming the sigh

of pork in the pan, bread baking, espresso
hissing over flame, eggs foamed and setting.
mama sits, back to stove, winter hair
pulling against the comb. she watches
the unwashed curtains, smells the rising
of a sea she can't stand to see. tired of fighting
the tangled covers, I tip-toe over cold floor,
stand goose-bumped at the window, hungry
for a clean plate of sky.

II

Sweet Home Alabama

Anniston — 1980

Mama mia, double *ma*, insistent
as a baby bird's mouth, the singsong
mia, trailing behind me, sinking
into the forest floor. My feet, fast,
tangling in my too-long skirt. Wild-
flowers. Blackberries. Briars.
I began to learn

English, sharp as my father's
knees, refused the *eccolo la*
of mother's stories. *Le parole*
began to unravel in my mouth,
dissolved back into letters, jumbled
and soggy as pastina. *Ah, bee, chee*,
became ABC. After lunch

she gave me a peach
and sent me out to play.
I pressed its calfskin
to my tongue, scraped
the flesh with my teeth,

tangy juice running down
my throat, down
my arms. I dug the stone out,
felt its ridges. A roughness.

I poked a hole in the freshly
seeded yard, pressed the dirt
flat with my palm, wishing
for more peaches, more
sweetness, to be born.

Lobster

Mother always made the bathwater
so hot it hurt, fire in my toes, sharp

bloom of lightning up each leg.
But I was old enough to know

not to say anything; not to scratch
the itch at the base of my knees.

One night, while she was scrubbing
my red skin with a washrag,

she got the far-away look
that meant trouble. *I cooked lobsters*

once, she said, *alive, the way you're*
supposed to, but when I dropped

them in the water, they screamed
like babies—my eyes, dull

as tarnished lead, scoop up
her milk-round cheek, twitch

of smile. She scrubbed
and scrubbed until I bled.

Joy

I got in trouble
for climbing trees,
rock walls, for
jumping on beds,
in streams, singing
at the table, for my
endless desire
to touch everything,
myself included—
all the things
that brought me joy
held punishment
inside them, like
a nesting doll filled
with stinging nettles,
or the wavering
delight of light
right before
an explosion.

The Other Mothers

how their voices droned—
like bumblebees, humming
in the hive. Warm honey,
suckled from the vine.
But when she approached,

their sweetness
hid a stinging. She limped
away, wounded. And soon,
stopped going. Wore
her bathrobe
night and day.

Living in the Land of Nod

The fairytales had taught me
about the women who fall asleep,

so of course I tried kissing
before all other things, but she

just slept and slept. For days,
weeks, months, or so it seemed.

I'd crawl into bed beside her,
listen for her breath, reassuring.

Sometimes I'd brush her hair,
like she was my biggest doll

to take care of, wisps framing
her face, but I could never

cover the white scalp
at the back, where her hair

parted, crushed from hours
of pressing against the pillow.

I hated that shock of white,
like a wound I might fall into.

So I'd lean in, tell her about my day,
where I'd been, who I'd seen. Wonder

if she could hear me, if my words
broke through her watery dreams—

I tried to make the moments
bolder, brighter, a shiny lure

that might tug her back
to the world of waking.

Bait

It was a story I'd laughed at
my entire life—that's how
it was told, a joke. My mother
barely able to tell it
between giggles—how they'd
sent her into the store
to ask for flies. *Flies?*
the grocer asked, confused.
Flies, she repeated.
For fishing? he asked. *Bait?*
No, she said in broken English,
moving her hand
to her mouth to mimic eating.
We put them in pudding,
delicious. And my father
and his uncle, hiding
behind a shelf, laughing,
and as she told it, all
of us, laughing again.

My Mother On Her Childhood

There was no pasta to boil. No
jam, no day-old bread.

I don't think you'll ever
be hungry enough to understand.

When My Mother Came Back From Her Nervous Breakdown, I Had Breasts

She hated them. They represented the time
she hadn't even known I was alive—

the weeks, months, maybe a year
spent crying, harming herself, pulling

out her hair, begging to die. Represented
the loss of one daughter and now, the future,

che fregatura, coming for another. That's
when she started to starve me. In my house,

when I was ten, there was no *clean your plate.*
Instead, there were Slim Fast shakes

for breakfast and lunch, and then
a *sensible dinner.* The woman on t.v.

made it sound so easy, but I was hungry.
No ice cream, no cakes, no cookies, or chips.

They were there for guests, but not for me.
In the summer, it was more intense: my mother

woke me up early each day to swim. A hundred
laps at seven a.m., another hundred at three. Walking

laps in between. Sit-ups the entire time
I was watching evening t.v. Once I refused,

and my father—trying to slap me—tripped,
sprained my ankle accidentally. I hadn't

even had my first period and already my body
was being punished for all the ways it would betray us.

If

you lose fifteen pounds
I'll buy you a new
wardrobe, a puppy,
I'll take you to Italy
to see my family. Fifty
dollars, a hundred,
I'll give you five
hundred dollars.

> *Can I take piano*
> *lessons, paint my room,*
> *start a garden?*

If you lose twenty, thirty,
maybe forty-five pounds.
A little more, a little
leaner, leaner still—

but it's never enough.
No matter how much less
and less and less
I am, I'm always
too much.

American

My mom wanted me
to be American, as seen
on t.v.: blonde, thin, rich.
She told me how women
on the soap operas
dressed. Was obsessed
with the lives of the people
in her *stories*—young
and restless, bold and
beautiful. She encouraged
drama, romances. *Love,*
she said, *is about power.*
Who loves most. Who
leaves first. She wanted me
to wear mascara, got mad
when I wouldn't. Combed
sun-in through my hair,
and when that didn't work,
just a little bleach. She forced me
to take gymnastics, dance,
to try out for cheerleader.
Tried to make me enter
pageants: *you could win,*
if you'd wear mascara. She'd
given up on being one of them—
put all her energy, her focus
on me, youngest daughter, last
chance for the American dream.

The Beguiled

At night, once my mother and I
had gone to bed, my father would sit
on his side of the love seat, sagging
from years of his weight, one arm's
fabric worn thin, the blue flick
of the tv, the sound turned up
to tinny, as he watched one
of the same three late night movies,
repeating for eternity, until he fell
asleep, snoring. My mother upstairs curled

on her side of the bed, lamp lit, cigarette
in the ashtray smoking, somewhere between
freshly lit and turned to ash: she burned
them like incense, an offering, as she read
Harlequin novels, one after the other, paperbacks
slipped off her library stack. And the sounds

of the Beguiled coming through the floorboards,
the women now lust-filled, now in love, now
seething, sawing through bone, and in her hands
she holds the man on his horse, bare-chested
on the edge of a cliff, or standing by a fence,
but it always ends with him picking her up,
taking her to bed.

Erasures

We ate soft pretzels, split
an Orange Julius
in the food court—
a special treat. Then,
fifteen minutes later,
when I couldn't fit
into the skirt she pulled
off the rack, she pinched
my belly fat, twisted,
saying nothing. Saying

everything. All day,
as we'd walked through
the mall, I'd try to hide,
slowed my walk, distanced
myself from her pink polyster
pants, flowered top, loud
cackle, Italian accent,
unforgiveable brashness—

I wanted to hold myself
separate, not get mixed up
in all the ways she didn't
fit in. I'd wanted to erase her.
And there she was, in
the fitting room, pinching,
blue-bruise forming,
on what she wanted
to erase of me.

Anatomy Lesson

grey slacks folded over wooden
hangers, shirts still wrapped
in dry-cleaner's plastic, ties

crammed wherever they would fit,
silk tongues flicking
from between the sports-coats,

the smell of tobacco and winter
trapped in the wool nap, buttons
shining like animal eyes:

parting the clothes, I found
a row of shoes, leather
showing the shape of toes,

their mouths stretched wide,
like catfish wanting to be fed,
and hidden beneath the shoes

a stack of magazines,
Hustler, filled with men, penises
thrown casually over their hairy

legs, as if they hadn't noticed
they were naked on a beach,
in the woods, on a leather couch—

and women, smiling over pricked
nipples, legs spread, sometimes
the V of their fingers stretching

to hold back their own flesh, inviting
me in. And then, there were both,
bodies intertwined like tree roots,

like snakes, like garden hoses. No.
Like none of these. Words left me,
kneeling, face flushed, green carpet

making my knees itch, the whole house
pulsing with silence, except
for the whisper of the turning page.

Backyard Baptisms

I was raised to believe
in the easy miracle
of water—slow screech
when I turned
the spigot, smell
of a wet penny, hiss
as the stream moved down
the rubber hose, swelled,
made a dancing
snake of it—coiling
and uncoiling—
the patio stained
with a slow
moving shadow
as the spray rainbowed
up my legs, soaked
the aquamarine swimsuit
I wore until mother
said it was indecent.

I took communion
in my mouth, the warm
water turning cool, tasting
like earth, like metal,
maybe a bit like blood. Like
that time my tooth
went through my bottom lip

and blood and blood
my entire mouth
was blood, and my mouth
was a blood-flower,
blooming.

Hunger

For years, there were no sweets
in the pantry, no salty snacks, no
junk of any kind. Then my parents

took over the youth group—
suddenly, cookies, candy, mixed
nuts, potato chips, twinkies, tang,

cans of cheese balls for other people's
kids. I would peel back the foil,
make a tiny hole in the plastic, plan

to eat just one, then unable
to control myself, two, four, handfuls,
my palms stained orange. Afraid

I'd get in trouble, I'd steal
the entire container. Then another.
One day I overheard my mother

on the phone with a call-in
therapy show—she had found
the wrappers, empty boxes, hidden

under my bed. She said, *My daughter,
has a problem*—her voice
in the living room and on tv,

echoing, back and forth, forever.
She hated my hunger—insatiable hole
she'd made to match her own.

Blush

I stood in front of my father,
too young to know how ugly
I was when I blushed—
the white splotches, the streaks
like burned fingers—
only old enough to know
the heat in my cheeks
when my father asked me *why*,
his army-issue glasses askew,
the frames so bold and black
and sure of themselves
that his skinny face seemed strange
and slant, *why*
would you kick that boy
there?

It was 1987. A Sunday,
because this was Sunday school,
and I couldn't tell my father
what that boy had called him,
the word he'd spit, his face twisted
so his teeth looked false,
couldn't even whisper the word
in my father's ear—

I didn't know, really, what it meant
but I knew it was meant to hurt
and his spittle burning my eyes
made me want to hurt him back, so yes,
I followed him into the boys' bathroom
and kicked him right in the place I felt that word

had come from, and he groaned, but I kicked
even harder, until a stall door creaked open—

I wouldn't think of this moment until years later,
2003, the same year my father died, when I stood
in the small security office I hadn't even known existed
in the back of grocery stores, looking down
at a metal desk, my mother's wrinkled purse splayed open,
a couple of gold-lined chocolate bars, some
candy wrappers, tissue strings,
and a small, silver moon of blush, unopened.

The Secret Room

In the dream—was it a dream? —
I found a room in the attic, cleared,
swept clean: bunk beds, a small
table, two chairs, an electric burner,
teakettle, potable water, canned
goods, all stacked and ordered—
enough food to hide for years. My father

after his father hanged himself
in prison, after the bad stepdad, lived
in the attic of his aunt's house, more
stranger than kin. And my mother

told me how her family hid
in the attic when the nazis came—
they'd shoot through the ceilings,
but never walk the two flights of stairs
to check if the cries they'd heard
were human. I look

at the beds, the card table, rows
and rows of canned goods, gleaming,
waiting for someone to open them.
This isn't a dream—it's the room built
from my parents' nightmares.

In the Dark

We practiced kissing
in a room so dark
it didn't matter
we were both girls,
just skin on skin,
warm, our lips
pressing together,
closed tight, no tongues,
pretending, and then,
like a Ouija board,
not sure whose hand
is pushing the planchette,
our bodies gliding
back and forth, smooth
and sinewy, muscling
together, tight, chest
against chest, smashing
breasts to feel
the beating,
and below, the jutting
hip bones, pelvis
against pelvis, crushing
the thin layers of cotton
between us, heat,
candy sweet, Bonne
Belle lip smackers
and a musky something,
moving between us,

like silk—we never
talked about it, never
told, just kept
to the shadows, shining
like moonflowers
in the dark.

Thirteen

I am thirteen, barely
in my body. I'm standing
in the bathroom door.
I feel like I need
to describe it to you:
the pink tiles, the powder blue
rug around the toilet, but no.
What you need to know
is how she held out her hand,
filled with beads, bright
beads, but not beads,
pills, and said *I'd kill myself*
if it wasn't
for you. If it wasn't

for you,
I'd kill myself, a handful
of pills, bright pills,
bees. She held out
what we needed to know. No.
The toilet, the powder blue rug
on pink tiles: I need to describe it
to feel—the mirror
I fell into. Standing
in the door of the bathroom,
barely in my body. I was thirteen
when my mother told me
she wanted to die.
I swallowed every pill.

Please

The morning after
I'd swallowed all her pills

I remember my mother
trying to make me drink

a latte—she always made me
coffee and milk on school

mornings, which was mostly
milk, just enough coffee

to tint, a trick, but this time
she made it darker and

darker still, and kept trying
to make me drink, but I

couldn't talk, couldn't open
my heavy-lidded eyes, the coffee

and milk running down
my chin, until finally I managed

to say *please mama, please,*
just let me sleep.

Homemade

When my mother came to see me in the hospital
she brought a tin of chocolate chip cookies. I sat

with the tin on my lap all during family therapy,
which is why we were there. The first session

since my attempted suicide, the first time
I'd seen them since being put in the ambulance. *Why,*

my mother asked, *is my daughter fat? What
are you feeding her?* I hadn't felt any different,

but as soon as she said it, the waistband of my skirt
started to pinch. *And yet,* my psychologist said,

*you brought cookies. Don't you think
you're sending mixed messages?* I sat, with the tin

on my lap, didn't say anything
as they discussed what I should/shouldn't eat. Assessed

my body, my ideal weight, my belly. I sat
next to my father, still and stern, also not speaking.

My mother had told me, more than once, how he'd come back
from Vietnam alive, but refused to say anything.

I'd come to believe it was how he'd survived—
by creating a fortress no one could penetrate.

I imagined myself gone, air, the tin floating, hovering
a couple of inches above the vinyl couch cushions.

The cookies inside, twenty tiny bombs, ticking. As soon
as my parents left, I ate all the cookies, then threw them up.

Solitary

I can't remember the crime
(stolen cereal, maybe? a
razor smuggled back to my
room after my shower?)
but the punishment
was being locked
in a glass box by myself,
nothing but a single bed,
so I slept. I woke to blood
all over me, went back
to sleep, woke up—
more blood, my jeans
now crusted with it,
down to my knees, like
I'd been wading in
a river of my own
making. I looked out
the window onto
the ward, wondered
if anyone would see,
bring me something
clean. No one did. So
I slept and bled, slept
and bled, bled
and slept again.

When My Mother Told Me
She Hadn't Loved My Father

I loved him even more, irrationally, heart swelling
over his freckles, his bald head, the way he bit
the side of his thumb until the skin bled. His Sunday
newspapers, the Western omelets he managed to make
so thin. How he'd come home from work, peel off his fatigues
in the kitchen, swim trunks beneath, come running—
cannonball—to join us. When she made me take dance,
gymnastics, try out for cheerleader, I wouldn't let her
come watch—only him. Once she went on a church retreat
and we were alone for a week—we didn't do anything special,
but for the first time in years, I could breathe. I started to wish
she'd leave, die, I didn't care. I wanted the peace
and quiet that came with her not being there. Wrote this
in my diary—a diary she read, she later told me. I never said
I hate you to her face, but it was right there, screaming
in red ink. Which is why, I guess, the united front
began. She told my father I was rotten, evil, manipulative,
caused fights between us. And the first time he hit me,
she didn't try to stop him and, in fact, seemed pleased.
And his hands—stinging palms, angry fists—I learned
to love even them.

Concessions

In the stand, slinging
dogs, wilting in the steam

while all around us, signs
promise chill—ICE THRILL, BLISS

BLIZZARD, COOL CRUSH—
an icy exoneration

that never reaches us. The wieners
sweat, the pretzels

turn to leather in their cage.
And every time I move

in that tight box, the manager
presses the bulge in his middle-aged

man jeans into me, full tilt, his hardness,
the heat, making me sick. I swallow

the bile, fill my orders
with a smile, until my shift

is done. Later, all us girls
sit in the concrete cut-outs,

our bare legs dangling
down the brick wall. We're high

above the spectator seats, unseen,
as we laugh at that prick, his tiny

prick, like a bee's prick, really, no

sting. We lean into each other, lick
BLEW RASPBERRY off our fingers,

watch the slow violence of fireworks,
noisy spectacle—useless—in our sky.

Post-War Love Story

Maybe the most important story
is the one I hated her for telling:
at its core, the man she loved (not

my father) how they strolled
in gardens, kissed for hours,
wild in moonlight, *true*

love, the burning kind, the one
she was meant to marry—
until everyone else on their street

got running water, indoor
toilets, electric lights—
the war was over, and somehow

the neighbors rebuilt, better
than ever. But her family's house
still crumbled, stank, still

the bunnies breeding beneath the stairs,
caged, watching for the itch of hunger
that meant one of their necks

would break. And him writing letters
from his regiment every day—
letters she knew would talk of after,

of marriage. But he had no job,
she had no dowry, and she hated
that house, falling in around them—

so she burned his letters, unopened,
unread, ran off to Paris,
where she met the American—

I planned to leave him
when I reached the States,
but then I fell in love, I guess.

This is the story I come from:
a pragmatism
born of war, of hunger,

the eyes under the stairs,
watching, and a little girl
who grew up knowing

sometimes you have to kill
the soft, warm, beautiful thing you love
in order to save yourself.

Saving Myself

Sometimes I'd sleep in my swimsuit
so I could stay in bed a little longer,

but the slip-slap of your house shoes
always came too soon. You wanted me

in the pool before the sun crossed
our yard, the water cool as blackbirds'

wings. I'd dive in, shocking my cells
all at once, while you worked your body down,

inch by inch. Beneath the vinyl-tinted waves
our bodies, blind contour drawings. We kept time

with laps, the well-practiced machinery
of us: you, an infinity of slow, lopsided circles,

jutting your chin above the water. I swam
in straight lines, single breaths, ignoring the distance

between the push of my feet and my fingertips
touching the wall. Eyes closed so I'd be surprised

when I hit. I was there swimming next to you
so I could save you, but I didn't know. Couldn't feel

the waves of your need. Below the surface
I'd sing, a silent film star strangling

out her last lines. I swam next to you,
until I swam away. Didn't even try

to save you. I was glad to leave.

III

Pane e Olio

Rome - 1993

My Zio Ugo came to get me
at the airport, hugged me

even though I barely
remembered him. He had

to bend over to kiss
my cheek, tall and thin,

egret of a man. He took
my bags, put them in his

blue sedan, and we sped off,
down the freeway, zipping in

and out of traffic, more near misses
than I could believe, all while

trying to speak to each other.
Italian was my first language,

but I'd lost it somewhere
in the woods of Alabama, kept

enough to eavesdrop on my parents.
Now I was trying to tell him

how I'd been dreaming of pane
e olio, babbling about how impossible

it was to get good bread
where we lived. *Pane e olio?*

he asked, fingers to his mouth,
miming the act of eating. I nodded,

and he screeched to a halt on the side
of the highway, other cars rushing past

us. *Vieni*, he said, gesturing for me
to follow. He went to the back of the car,

opened the trunk and pulled out a huge loaf
of pane casareccio, a serrated knife,

a jug of oil, shining green in the afternoon
light. He even had a small pinch of salt,

and right there, on the side of the autostrada,
he made me pane e olio, a welcome to Italy.

Jetlagged, yet hyperaware, it felt like a dream.
I'd just arrived and already I was being fed.

L'americana

I move among them
close enough to touch

the man with stiff silver whiskers
wearing a hand wrung
linen suit, *Corriere
della Sera*
tucked under his arm
as he leans
on his brass-handled cane

the woman in mourning,
matted black wool
in August heat, her bulging cart
difficult for her to maneuver
through the crowded streets

the young man,
smoking
outside il tabaccaio,
his black curls shining—

I want to rest my palm flat
on his hairy chest
feel his heart beat
beneath his crucifix

I want to touch
but do not

not even the soft fig
the hollow-mouthed woman
holds out to me

this is my mother's country
somewhere, deep inside, mine
but it is my father's hiss I hear
look but don't touch look
but don't touch anything

on the walls of the buildings
surrounding us
someone has painted silhouettes,
thick, black strokes
turned to life-sized shadows

their silence, their
terrible stillness

as I round corners,
approach shops—

even in profile
I see them peeking—

sometimes I lean against them
shrink back, try to find the vanishing point.

Is this where people go
when they are too separate
to be useful, but not beautiful enough
to be statues?

Standing Woman

Gaston Lachaise, 1932

The thing about seeing breasts
that look almost exactly
like my breasts

cast in bronze, yet somehow
alarmingly real, these parts
of me I'd always hated—

>   their weight, pulling them
>   down, pendulous fruit, suspended

>   like two lost planets ready
>   to collide in some far-off

>   galaxy. The belly, a bottomless
>   bowl, stretching—

is I must admit, as I walk
around and around this version
of me, that there's something here

that could be called *beauty*. If not,
why do I want to lean in, and touch
the tip of my tongue to this sculpture?

The Casting, Imagined

It must've been hard
not to squirm
while he rubbed Vaseline
over her breasts, nipples.

She gripped the ropes
he'd given her to hold onto,
kept her back
to the wall, held her scream-

laugh inside her—
sweet torture.
Then came the plaster
and burlap bandages, soft

and scratchy woven
together, the slow
layering over her large
mounds, rippling like lakes

as he smoothed them,
entirely focused on her shape,
on the shape he was making. Her
nipples, sharp as daggers

ready to kill, as he moved
to the crease beneath, her angry
beauty mark, flaring red
on pale skin. The side of his hand

swept the layers of cloth
over her rib cage, then he gripped
with both hands, smoothing,
sculpting, as he moved down

to her belly. And yes,
she moaned a bit,
as the cold plaster reacted,
started to heat up, and her

—burning—inside this second
skin. And yes, his closeness,
his scent, his hands, all over,
his lips so near—

But all she could do was watch
as the plaster hardened, began
to set. She dreamed of the moment
she would break free

from this mold he'd made,
walk out of this plaster cage—
and take her turn
making art out of him.

L'italiana

I move among them
close enough to touch—I've just turned twenty,

but have I lived a single minute?—my fingers trace
the rough bricks, mortared

faces. I take
the fig,   suck
the fruit from its skin

I approach the smoking boy,   ask him
for a ride on his vespa,   my palms

rest softly
on his muscled
arms—   I have no idea

where we're going
but I know I'm done

living like a stranger
within the borders
of my own body—   I lean in,

        squeeze my thighs,

    tight

        on every turn.

Curfew

I was living in a boarding house
run by nuns, when my date
dropped me off, leaned in
for the expected good night
kiss and then, unexpectedly,

rubbed my right breast, over
my blouse, in hard, fast,
vicious circles with the palm
of his hand, so sudden,
so surprising, I didn't

pull back—the friction, the dizzy
heat, the flush of pleasure I'd
never felt when being felt—
and that night I learned a lesson
about my own body, learned

my breasts needed rough love,
as a train roared up my thighs, exploded
through the mountains of me, right
there, on the steps of the Figlie
di San Giuseppe, ten minutes
before convent bells sang me in.

Still-Life: Window with a View of Other Windows

This city's
too hot
for sleeping,

so I lean out
the window,
lift my head, howl

smoke rings
     to the god
of 3 A.M.—

morse code
or prayer?—
either way

his light clicks
on—him
gilded

in his window
frame, one hand
holding a knife

the other
a piece of fruit:
listen: it isn't enough
                           to say *orange*
                           I need you to see

the orb, burning
and me, alone
in the city, pulsing—

how I need
to feel
something real,

its weight
in my hand,   flesh
on my lips—
(and how determined
 I can get

                  when I want

even if
 it's my own
undoing)   but tonight

with a million miles
of brick
between us

I just watch
as he carves
his spiral staircase, watch

as it neons
into night, knowing
there's no such thing

as still life, knowing
I will climb
and climb and climb.

David

Michaelangelo, 1504

What I wanted—

nothing more/nothing
less—

was to hold
the most private
part of him
in my hand,

to see
how it fit,

to feel it pulse
to life
in the warmth
of my grip.

Pomegranate

I split open
in my sleep
  wake
 to blood
on my sheets, my
forehead, my
fingers, knuckle-
deep   tell me

what kind of strange
dream
  is this—
touching myself
without the pleasure
of remembering
whose name
I cried out, whose
back
I scratched, whose
tongue
my body arched
to meet, whose hips
my hips
  crashed
  and crashed
  and crashed
against? Tender
all that's left
come morning—
  pulsing—

                    Once
I picked up
a pomegranate,
split it
   with the tip
of my knife, juice
running down
the sides, then
   I submerged

the fruit
in water, my hands
ripping the skin,
its jewels spilling

into the sink,

into the palms
of my hands, greedily
        gathering
every seed

   and for days

my hands were stained
red, mark
of fire, a sign
for all to see
of my feverish

fiendish

hunger

Bocca della Verità

He only likes Rome
at one in the morning,
when the marketplace is empty,
and he can hear each tick
of my heels tapping stone.

We walk the labyrinth
around the piazza, shop
the dim storefronts.
When he kisses me, I feel

the mannequins watching, trees
made of alabaster, their ghost
faces hopeful, their arms
flung wide—

shadows spring from darkness—
big, black dogs
look more like wolves
to me, in my red riding hood
cape, but he says *they're just looking*
for a trash can
to knock over, for *a piece*
of meat
to gobble up.

We make our way
to the colosseum, starving
for spectacle—take turns
being lions, roaring
and pouncing. Argue

over who's mastered
the clean kill.

At dawn we stand
where everybody stands, mouth
of truth, a lie detector
with teeth. I trace the furrows
in his scraggly beard, laugh
as I lean in. But he's not happy
until he forces my hand
deep in its mouth, asks—

The Day Before I Found Out
I Was Pregnant

he took me to buy the CD I wanted, Mia
Martini. I asked the man behind the counter
if they had it: he walked me over to a glass case,
unlocked it, handed me the CD, and I bought it.
Then we left. As we drove back down
the mountain, I counted the stone houses
stacking up in the side mirror while he swerved,
ranted about how I'd almost had sex
with the man in the store right in front of him.
He kept me up all night, following me
from room to room, smashing things,
cutting up my clothing. I tried talking,
tried ignoring him—finally I started packing.
When everything was loaded in the car,
he started sobbing, begged me to stay—he was
so sorry, so afraid to lose me. I was tired.
Had never been that tired. And in the morning,
there was a single spot of blood in my panties.
No more came.

Catacombs

It smells like the cellar where nonna
kept ice cream. It smells like things should
grow, but the air's too cold, the ground
too hard to push life into. We take dumb steps,

ants inching through tunnels, negative
architecture: walls, floor, ceiling, tomb
markers with names chiseled in all caps.
It's the remains that stand out: moon sliver

of rib, skulls ready to talk, skeletons still
bleeding in rust-colored cloth. And us. Like them,
but clinging. I stop to touch one, but you take
my extended hand, pull me into smaller

and smaller spaces, until we're stooped,
then crawling on all fours. We emerge in a chapel,
where first sun forces itself through lead glass,
quilts our ashen faces. You kiss me and I taste

all the dead things you want to bury in me (bound men
rescued from furnace-flames, Noah riding the waters
that drowned the neighborhood children, Daniel
encircled by lions, standing uneaten). I marry you anyway.

Birth

By birth we mean beginning to reform,
a thing's becoming other than it was.
OVID

Pressure between my legs, an ache
an urge to push. I tell the nurse
I think he's here. She
laughs. *First time?*
Believe me, it's not
that easy. She checks,
looks startled—*Don't push,*
she says, *the doctor's not here yet.*
I clench my muscles
against my instincts. Fire
shoots through me. My mother,
beside me says *Spingere. Spingere.*
Tells me, *the nurses know*
how to deliver a baby—
they just want the doctor here
to cut you. So I push,
holding the hand of the woman
who'd once done this same,
impossible splitting for me—
and as my body opened, I

released all the anger, all
the grief—everything
I'd been holding. And when
my son screamed his way
into the room, it sounded exactly
like a bridge
arching the air between us.

Birth

Except, it happened like this:

Spingere, spingere, my mother said,
the nurses know
how to deliver a baby—
they just want the doctor here
so he can cut you. I

didn't push. I held
my legs together, held
my son inside me
for over an hour.

I trusted the man
who walked in, grabbed
a scalpel, and cut
slit-to-slit, didn't
even look at me, my blood
pouring into a bucket
as he pulled the baby out, walked
away from me. Trusted him

more than my own mother.
My own body. And when
he stitched me up, he stitched
all my rage, all my pain
inside me. But my mother—
my mother—held me.

Chiaroscuro

Moth, flittering pulse against our porch light,
trying to push through
the glass sphere, not knowing
the bare bulb will singe
your dusty wings—why

are you so frantic? Why not learn
from the seedling,
too soon to tell
if it's tulip or onion,
just green blade slicing
through earth

or the snake, craving
the sun-warm stone,
bulging free
from its leather shell.

Moth, I remember frantic need—
baby shouldering his way
into the white scream
of our hospital room.

Yes, we all push toward the light.

But a plant keeps the dark
in its roots, veins throbbing
through cold soil,

and snakes burrow back
behind logs, blood-thick
and somnolent,

and my son is finally asleep
in the soft night of his nursery,
while I sit outside, awake

in the prayer of my body,
its musky dark, flickering
mind, steady sound
of my own stubborn pulsing.

Self-Portrait as Light at the End of the Tunnel

You know I'm nervous. Not claustrophobic, just unable to stand
stale air. When you roll down the windows, slap me in the face
with January, I know it's time. You say *breathe deep*, as if I need
your directive. Windows seal shut as we enter the tunnel, the longest
in the world. You hold my hand, push down on my pulse point. I hate
the smell of old oil, urine, the way the light makes us look skeletal—
at dead center it's too many miles in either direction—you tell me
the mountain was a hiding place for the Swiss during war, a secret hollow
carved for the entire village to swarm inside. I say *I'd face my attacker*,
but looking at you, green in dashboard glow—it isn't true. Up ahead
a ring of light, like a lid slipped off a jar of honey. I taste the wild air,
let it consume me. I'm tired of holding winter in my chest.

Self-Portrait as Woman Waking

Wives wear their hair short. I pinned
    it up, out of sight, convinced you
    there was no need for the knife. *No red*

lipstick. Don't step so loud. No locked doors.
    What are you always writing about? Is it
    me? I stopped writing. Stopped

doing almost everything. Everything
    made you mad. And when you were mad
    What you see belongs to me—those

cigarettes, food, you have nothing—
    Once you forced me out on the street, locked
    the door. I couldn't speak German, couldn't

leave—you had the baby inside. I could hear him
    crying, hungry, my breasts pinpricks,
    my blouse soaked with milk. Sour. But when you

let me back in, you were nice again. I started to doubt
    my own memory. Each day, I'd take your shirts
    off the clothesline, hide in the steam room,

where the hiss and sighs of my iron could
    at least smooth something. I kept
    the baby with me, afraid to leave him.

When I found coins in your pockets, I'd steal them,
    hide them in my shoes. One afternoon,
    I saw myself in the mirror—on my hands

and knees hiding Deutsche marks, and suddenly
    I saw clearly. I put my shoes on, walked
    to the corner, called my mother from the payphone—

she told me a plane ticket would be waiting for me
    the next day at the airport, didn't ask
    a single question. *Come home*, she says.

Sirens

He kept me locked in
all night. Never touched me,

but wouldn't let me go.
He wanted me to know

he could—hold me,
hurt me—if he wanted. If

I screamed, no one
would hear. I can't remember

if he said this, or if
I just knew—the way girls

just know so many things. *Show
don't tell,* the teacher said. No.

It wasn't that no one would hear—
it's that they wouldn't care.

They wouldn't do
anything. That's

what I knew. My father
taught me that—my father's

belt, my father's fists—
My black eye. My favorite

teacher finding me
on the floor of the bathroom

and saying *if you tell me,*
I'll have no choice,

and I knew she meant *don't.*
So I didn't. But back on the street,

after he turned the deadbolt,
let me leave, I hear the sirens scream

and my voice rises to join them
in furious revelry.

Your Hands Hover on the Edge of the World

1.

Snapshot of first steps: He stumbles over winter grass,
arms flailing. He's wearing a padded jumper and white
leather lace-ups. His legs are painfully bowed.

On the left edge, your hands hover, severed
at the wrist. Open hands, dragonfly
mid-flight.

I'm not in the picture. I'm taking the picture.

It's impossible to capture the short distance
between us—how he crosses it, grabs my leg.

2.

You asked if I'd come back. I said *maybe*,
and meant it, sure once I left I'd remember
only good. He was sleep-heavy in my arms,
my shoulder shrugging his lips into a wet pout.
We could only bring two bags, so I left you
at the airport holding the collapsible baby bed.

3.

He woke after take-off and never went back to sleep.
He wanted to walk, so we walked the narrow confines
of that plane. For ten hours, I held his hands, felt
his steps solidify. The night we left behind
became grey morning.

4.

What I'd called bonds were only cobwebs, caught
in broom-straw, swept into gossamer threads,
microscopic specks of dust, then nothing but air. Air!

5.

When I told you I wasn't coming back
you disappeared in thin—

6.

He walked each day on the beach:
curved bones straightening, calves
elongating. Soon he needed
no hands.

7.

He doesn't remember grass stains,
the smell of fall dirt, pebble-dents
pulsing in his palms—

doesn't remember the airport,
the baby bed, you.

8.

I barely do.

9.

He fills his bed now, more man than boy,
but sometimes his lips still pout when he dreams.
His nose is his nose; his chest, his chest.
His long, tapered fingers continue
long after mine end.

Remembering Only Bad

We had olive trees we spent entire days
plucking fruit from, our bare arms

muscled and bronzed. We planted strawberries,
watched new potatoes sprout

from the eyes of old ones. And yet, I only want
the dust my feet kicked up in the yard, the way

the crumbling ruins behind the main house
blended into the monochrome landscape,

the animals so thin I could see their ribs
slicing their tightly stretched hides. How

mean you were to them. I don't want
to remember anything that bloomed, that

grew, anything that could be called living.
Except maybe the wild artichokes—

how I peeled back the spiny leaves,
found scorpions nestled close to the heart.

Aerie

Oak planks swept smooth. The creak
you've come to know. Corner desk,

unpolished. A lamp turned low.
Curtains catch and fall, like beats

of breath. I've emptied my suitcase.
Ironed all my clothes into stiff skins

I no longer want to wear. I let my silk
robe slip open, stand at the porcelain sink,

waiting for the water to warm—
steam rises in little puffs. The soap,

green as jadestone, perfectly coiled
in the groove of its dish. Wind pushes

sun through the screens, pulsing
like hummingbirds into the room,

and I want to call everyone I know
and ask *is it light where you are, is it light?*

Trap

I wasn't there when the coyote grabbed my cat,
I only saw the aftermath—puncture wounds
on each flank, craters barreling through muscle,
the jagged tear where he ripped himself free
from its teeth. And in the weeks that followed,
stitches, the puckered skin, angry and red.
The purple road of scar, disappearing between
the bristle of new fur, until all that was left
was the shiver running down his back
whenever we heard the coyote's cry, fulvous ghost
roaming our neighborhood each night. The nurse
described my father's scream—a wail, really—
rounding the corner of the ICU like a siren. She
described it because none of us were there
to hear it, and for months after, as we turned
his body, checked his feeding tube, I tried
to imagine it. When I left him sitting on the edge

of his hospital bed, he was he and I was I, and I didn't
hug him goodbye, because even with his mouth
drooping, even with his left arm limp in his lap,
I didn't trust him. Didn't trust my body
near his body, as if his weakness were a trap
I might fall into. But after—after that scream,
after the long weeks of radio silence, I rubbed lotion
on his feet, his legs, his arms. Cared for him
as if he were an infant. His hands, once large,
now shriveled like old roots dug up from the garden;
his neatly clipped nails now jagged, caked with grime.
And I remembered those hands setting beautiful tables
on holidays, porcelain and polished silver, folding

each napkin into a triangle, or once, swans, their necks
bobbing from our crystal wine glasses. His hands
painting ceramics, carving pumpkins, patting my back
when he comforted me, fixing things. His hands
pushing me under in the pool, playing for hours
after work, catching me when I jumped in. His hands
lifting me from the bed of the station wagon, going back
for the dozen stuffed animals I'd insisted on bringing
with me, tucking each one in beside me. His hands
holding my son, so gently. And I took a tissue from its box,
caressed his head, his face, his neck, his chest, trailing
down each arm, soft as a breeze over each hand. This tenderness
I showed him was not mercy. It was not even forgiveness.
It was love, holding on to two truths at once. It was
the opposite of the coyote's howl, the hole, and I felt like god,
glorious in her gentleness, when after weeks of silence
he spoke my name, said *Danielle, do the velvet touch again,*
and I did, my touch softer, and softer,
until the trap's jaw opened—

First Fruit of the Season

I want to stick to the trail, but my son says
the best ones grow out of reach. He tugs me

into brambles, scratches etching
my bare legs, tree limbs making birds' nests

of my hair. We pick our fingers purple,
leave behind only what the ants claimed

first. As our basket creaks heavy, the rose-
vine handle pricks my arm. We go back

to our pine-box kitchen, mansard roof
forcing my shoulders curved. He washes

berries in the sink, blue buoys floating
on water. I prepare the dented pots,

place wide-mouthed jars upside down
on tea towels, seals ready to snap

in place. The saucepan rattles and hisses,
steam covering everything like a spell.

When the fruit boils down, there's only
enough for one jar, too small to shelve,

so we sit in the blue dusk, eat
the delicious fruit still warm.

Mending

Piece by piece, I recreate the scene: the sky,
the well, the wall, the shade tree. The field

reforming, porcelain puzzle pieces fitting,
gold joining wheat, wildflowers, resetting—

landscape with alternate ending—stretching

around the corners of the bowl, now newly
whole, scars shining. I place each bird, each

bluebonnet—the broken, bonded. Again
able to hold its own. And in some future kitchen—

mine? ours? — a handful of cherries, a set
of keys, magnolia blooms—first signs of spring.

Acknowledgments

A pot of espresso, an abundance of biscotti, and my sincere gratitude to the editors of the journals in which some of these poems have appeared, at times in different forms: *apt Magazine, DMQ Review, First Inkling, Incessant Pipe, MER, Midway Journal, Molecule: a tiny lit mag, Paper Nautilus,* and *Southern Women's Review*

"Chiaroscuro" was the winner of the Vella Poetry Prize; "Nostra Donna Del Cielo" was a finalist in the *Winning Writers'* War Poetry Contest; "Mending" appeared in *After a Line by Anne Bradstreet,* curated and edited by Christy Pottroff; and "Portrait of a Woman in Kitchen" was reprinted in *Verse Daily* and appeared on the Red Line as part of the "Poetry on the T" project for Mass Poetry.

These poems were written with financial support from the Brother Thomas Foundation, the Mass Cultural Council, the New England Poetry Club, the Rona Jaffe Foundation, and the St. Botolph Club Foundation. Their generous gifts kept the lights on (literally and metaphorically) during some tough times, and I am incredibly grateful. I also received loving support from the Fine Arts Work Center, Mass Poetry, the Palm Beach Poetry Festival, and the Salem Athenaeum. Thank you for the work you do to provide artists with time and space to write and connect.

Thank you to *Bordighera Press* for selecting my manuscript and bringing my dream to life. Nicholas Grosso, working with you has been a pleasure. Grazie mille.

To the teachers who offered mentorship and guidance throughout the years: Polly Pitts, who designed a creative writing class just for me in high school, allowing me to sit in a room by myself and write poems; Pitt Harding, whose creative writing class I took "for fun" my last year in college—only to find it was a portal to an entirely different future; Joyce Peseroff and Lloyd Schwartz, for welcoming me to UMass Boston and giving me everything I needed to grow; Suji Kwock Kim, for intense (and much needed) lessons on craft; and Andrea Cohen and Jill McDonough, for teaching me to live the poems. "You must change your life," and indeed, you changed mine.

I'm honored to write, live, and work among so many brilliant and generous people, whether my UMass Boston cohort, the Salem Writers Group, Incessant Pipe, my colleagues at UNH, or all the folks I've met here and there along the way. I cannot possibly list you all, but in a world that feels very performative at times, I am so thankful to have found true community. Special thanks to Diannely Antigua, Lis Horowitz, Jennifer Martelli, Jill McDonough, Dawn Paul, J.D. Scrimgeour, and Cindy Veach for helping this book take shape. Extra special thanks to Angela Voras-Hills, my first and favorite reader, and my PFF; to M.P. Carver and Clay Ventre, who kept sending up flares whenever I thought I'd completely lost my way, in poetry and in life —and Clay, again, for the editorial advice and gentle push this book (and its author) needed to make it to the other side; and Susanna Baird—there are not enough words, my friend, for all you mean to me.

To Joshua Burford, Star Burgess, Karyn Coughlin, Dawn Price Cox, Monica Ellison Haynes, Pamela Haskew Brunson, Trace Fleming-Trice, Jason Roach, Kelli Coughlin Schoen, Leda Swann, and Chris Williamson: thank you for your friendship during the hard years of these poems, and beyond.

Michael Jones and Patricia Watson, you are the best big brother and sister a little girl could ask for. Your love and support keep me on this earth.

Thank you to Josh, Alex, and Andrew for moving across the country—uprooting your own lives—so I could follow my poetry dreams. This book wouldn't exist without you, and I wouldn't be quite the same either.

And thank you to my mother, Mafalda Luigia Felicetti Jones, for telling me your stories, and for making me strong enough to tell my own.

About the Author

DANIELLE JONES is a poet, artist, and educator. She holds an MFA from UMass Boston. Her work has appeared in *Beloit Poetry Journal*, *Best New Poets*, *Consequence Magazine*, *Memorious*, *Rattle*, and elsewhere. She is a recipient of a Rona Jaffe Writer's Award, a St. Botolph's Club Emerging Artist Award, a Mass Cultural Council Artist Fellowship, and a Brother Thomas Foundation Fellowship. She teaches writing at the University of New Hampshire, where she directs the Nossrat Yassini Poetry Festival and manages *YAS Press*.

VIA FOLIOS

A refereed book series dedicated to the culture of Italians and Italian Americans.

ROSEMARY CAPPELLO. *Wonderful Disaster*. Vol. 142. Poetry.
B. AMORE. *Journeys on the Wheel*. Vol. 141. Poetry.
ALDO PALAZZESCHI. *The Manifestos of Aldo Paluzzeschi*. Vol 140. Literature.
ROSS TALARICO. *The Reckoning*. Vol 139. Poetry.
MICHELLE REALE. *Season of Subtraction*. Vol 138. Poetry.
MARISA FRASCA. *Wild Fennel*. Vol 137. Poetry.
RITA ESPOSITO WATSON. *Italian Kisses*. Vol. 136. Memoir.
SARA FRUNER. *Bitter Bites from Sugar Hills*. Vol. 135. Poetry.
KATHY CURTO. *Not for Nothing*. Vol. 134. Memoir.
JENNIFER MARTELLI. *My Tarantella*. Vol. 133. Poetry.
MARIA TERRONE. *At Home in the New World*. Vol. 132. Essays.
GIL FAGIANI. *Missing Madonnas*. Vol. 131. Poetry.
LEWIS TURCO. *The Sonnetarium*. Vol. 130. Poetry.
JOE AMATO. *Samuel Taylor's Hollywood Adventure*. Vol. 129. Novel.
BEA TUSIANI. *Con Amore*. Vol. 128. Memoir.
MARIA GIURA. *What My Father Taught Me*. Vol. 127. Poetry.
STANISLAO PUGLIESE. *A Century of Sinatra*. Vol. 126. Popular Culture.
TONY ARDIZZONE. *The Arab's Ox*. Vol. 125. Novel.
PHYLLIS CAPELLO. *Packs Small Plays Big*. Vol. 124. Literature.
FRED GARDAPHÉ. *Read 'em and Reap*. Vol. 123. Criticism.
JOSEPH A. AMATO. *Diagnostics*. Vol 122. Literature.
DENNIS BARONE. *Second Thoughts*. Vol 121. Poetry.
OLIVIA K. CERRONE. *The Hunger Saint*. Vol 120. Novella.
GARIBLADI M. LAPOLLA. *Miss Rollins in Love*. Vol 119. Novel.
JOSEPH TUSIANI. *A Clarion Call*. Vol 118. Poetry.
JOSEPH A. AMATO. *My Three Sicilies*. Vol 117. Poetry & Prose.
MARGHERITA COSTA. *Voice of a Virtuosa and Coutesan*. Vol 116. Poetry.
NICOLE SANTALUCIA. *Because I Did Not Die*. Vol 115. Poetry.
MARK CIABATTARI. *Preludes to History*. Vol 114. Poetry.
HELEN BAROLINI. *Visits*. Vol 113. Novel.
ERNESTO LIVORNI. *The Fathers' America*. Vol 112. Poetry.
MARIO B. MIGNONE. *The Story of My People*. Vol 111. Non-fiction.
GEORGE GUIDA. *The Sleeping Gulf*. Vol 110. Poetry.
JOEY NICOLETTI. *Reverse Graffiti*. Vol 109. Poetry.
GIOSE RIMANELLI. *Il mestiere del furbo*. Vol 108. Criticism.
LEWIS TURCO. *The Hero Enkidu*. Vol 107. Poetry.
AL TACCONELLI. *Perhaps Fly*. Vol 106. Poetry.
RACHEL GUIDO DEVRIES. *A Woman Unknown in Her Bones*. Vol 105. Poetry.
BERNARD BRUNO. *A Tear and a Tear in My Heart*. Vol 104. Non-fiction.
FELIX STEFANILE. *Songs of the Sparrow*. Vol 103. Poetry.
FRANK POLIZZI. *A New Life with Bianca*. Vol 102. Poetry.
GIL FAGIANI. *Stone Walls*. Vol 101. Poetry.
LOUISE DESALVO. *Casting Off*. Vol 100. Fiction.
MARY JO BONA. *I Stop Waiting for You*. Vol 99. Poetry.
RACHEL GUIDO DEVRIES. *Stati zitt, Josie*. Vol 98. Children's Literature. $8
GRACE CAVALIERI. *The Mandate of Heaven*. Vol 97. Poetry.

MARISA FRASCA. *Via incanto*. Vol 96. Poetry.
DOUGLAS GLADSTONE. *Carving a Niche for Himself.* Vol 95. History.
MARIA TERRONE. *Eye to Eye*. Vol 94. Poetry.
CONSTANCE SANCETTA. *Here in Cerchio*. Vol 93. Local History.
MARIA MAZZIOTTI GILLAN. *Ancestors' Song*. Vol 92. Poetry.
MICHAEL PARENTI. *Waiting for Yesterday: Pages from a Street Kid's Life*.
   Vol 90. Memoir.
ANNIE LANZILLOTTO. *Schistsong*. Vol 89. Poetry.
EMANUEL DI PASQUALE. *Love Lines*. Vol 88. Poetry.
CAROSONE & LOGIUDICE. *Our Naked Lives*. Vol 87. Essays.
JAMES PERICONI. *Strangers in a Strange Land: A Survey of Italian-Language
   American Books*.Vol 86. Book History.
DANIELA GIOSEFFI. *Escaping La Vita Della Cucina*. Vol 85. Essays.
MARIA FAMÀ. *Mystics in the Family*. Vol 84. Poetry.
ROSSANA DEL ZIO. *From Bread and Tomatoes to Zuppa di Pesce "Ciambotto"*.
   Vol. 83. Memoir.
LORENZO DELBOCA. *Polentoni*. Vol 82. Italian Studies.
SAMUEL GHELLI. *A Reference Grammar*. Vol 81. Italian Language.
ROSS TALARICO. *Sled Run*. Vol 80. Fiction.
FRED MISURELLA. *Only Sons*. Vol 79. Fiction.
FRANK LENTRICCHIA. *The Portable Lentricchia*. Vol 78. Fiction.
RICHARD VETERE. *The Other Colors in a Snow Storm*. Vol 77. Poetry.
GARIBALDI LAPOLLA. *Fire in the Flesh*. Vol 76 Fiction & Criticism.
GEORGE GUIDA. *The Pope Stories*. Vol 75 Prose.
ROBERT VISCUSI. *Ellis Island*. Vol 74. Poetry.
ELENA GIANINI BELOTTI. *The Bitter Taste of Strangers Bread*. Vol 73. Fiction.
PINO APRILE. *Terroni*. Vol 72. Italian Studies.
EMANUEL DI PASQUALE. *Harvest*. Vol 71. Poetry.
ROBERT ZWEIG. *Return to Naples*. Vol 70. Memoir.
AIROS & CAPPELLI. *Guido*. Vol 69. Italian/American Studies.
FRED GARDAPHÉ. *Moustache Pete is Dead! Long Live Moustache Pete!*.
   Vol 67. Literature/Oral History.
PAOLO RUFFILLI. *Dark Room/Camera oscura*. Vol 66. Poetry.
HELEN BAROLINI. *Crossing the Alps*. Vol 65. Fiction.
COSMO FERRARA. *Profiles of Italian Americans*. Vol 64. Italian Americana.
GIL FAGIANI. *Chianti in Connecticut*. Vol 63. Poetry.
BASSETTI & D'ACQUINO. *Italic Lessons*. Vol 62. Italian/American Studies.
CAVALIERI & PASCARELLI, Eds. *The Poet's Cookbook*. Vol 61. Poetry/Recipes.
EMANUEL DI PASQUALE. *Siciliana*. Vol 60. Poetry.
NATALIA COSTA, Ed. *Bufalini*. Vol 59. Poetry.
RICHARD VETERE. *Baroque*. Vol 58. Fiction.
LEWIS TURCO. *La Famiglia/The Family*. Vol 57. Memoir.
NICK JAMES MILETI. *The Unscrupulous*. Vol 56. Humanities.
BASSETTI. ACCOLLA. D'AQUINO. *Italici: An Encounter with Piero Bassetti*.
   Vol 55. Italian Studies.
GIOSE RIMANELLI. *The Three-legged One*. Vol 54. Fiction.

LUIGI RUSTICHELLI, Ed. *Seminario sulla drammaturgia.*
   Vol 14. Theater/Essays.
FRED GARDAPHÈ. *Moustache Pete is Dead! Long Live Moustache Pete!.*
   Vol 13. Oral Literature.
JONE GAILLARD CORSI. *Il libretto d'autore. 1860 - 1930.* Vol 12. Criticism.
HELEN BAROLINI. *Chiaroscuro: Essays of Identity.* Vol 11. Essays.
PICARAZZI & FEINSTEIN, Eds. *An African Harlequin in Milan.*
   Vol 10. Theater/Essays.
JOSEPH RICAPITO. *Florentine Streets & Other Poems.* Vol 9. Poetry.
FRED MISURELLA. *Short Time.* Vol 8. Novella.
NED CONDINI. *Quartettsatz.* Vol 7. Poetry.
ANTHONY JULIAN TAMBURRI, Ed. *Fuori: Essays by Italian/American
   Lesbiansand Gays.* Vol 6. Essays.
ANTONIO GRAMSCI. P. Verdicchio. Trans. & Intro. *The Southern Question.*
   Vol 5. Social Criticism.
DANIELA GIOSEFFI. *Word Wounds & Water Flowers.* Vol 4. Poetry. $8
WILEY FEINSTEIN. *Humility's Deceit: Calvino Reading Ariosto Reading Calvino.*
   Vol 3. Criticism.
PAOLO A. GIORDANO, Ed. *Joseph Tusiani: Poet. Translator. Humanist.*
   Vol 2. Criticism.
ROBERT VISCUSI. *Oration Upon the Most Recent Death of Christopher Columbus.*
   Vol 1. Poetry.

www.ingramcontent.com/pod-product-compliance
Lightning Source LLC
Chambersburg PA
CBHW020206090426
42734CB00008B/956